BUILDINGS

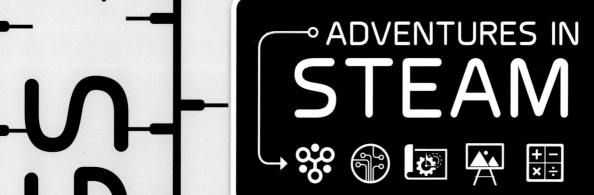

ADVENTURES IN STEAM

Izzi Howell

Fact Finders®

CAPSTONE PRESS
a capstone imprint

Fact Finders Books are published by Capstone Press,
1710 Roe Crest Drive, North Mankato, Minnesota 56003
www.mycapstone.com

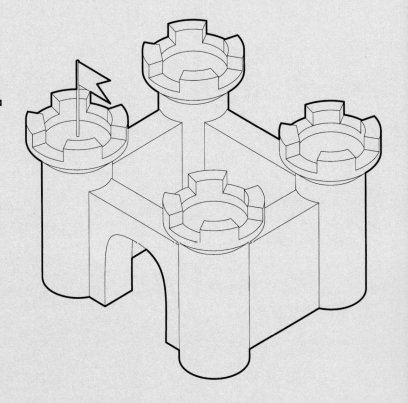

LIBRARY OF CONGRESS CATALOGING-IN-PUBLICATION DATA

Library of Congress Cataloging-in-Publication data is available on the Library of Congress website.
978-1-5435-3224-1 (library binding)
978-1-5435-3298-2 (paperback)
978-1-5435-3550-1 (eBook PDF)

Summary: Closely ties the construction and engineering processes to the STEAM Initiative. Examines structures from concept and design to the materials needed and their final construction. Explores how buildings and architecture have evolved over time, and explains how engineers balance forces to support skyscrapers, bridges, tunnels, and other amazing structures.

EDITORIAL CREDITS

Series editor: Izzi Howell
Designer: Rocket Design (East Anglia) Ltd
Illustrations: Rocket Design (East Anglia) Ltd
In-house editor: Julia Bird/Catherine Brereton

PHOTO CREDITS

Alamy: Historic Collection 42; iStock: pa_YON 12b, kpalimski 15, HomoCosmicos 18b, rmnunes 23l, ValeryEgorov 23r, Ismailciydem 24tr, erlucho 25t, Agenturfotograf 26b, nidwlw 27, pics-xl 28, hippostudio 33tr, david franklin 35br, espiegle 39t, oversnap 39bl, Leonid Andronov 41; Julian Baker: 30b and 43; Shutterstock: alice-photo cover and title page, Ray_of_Light 3 and 12-13t, Dan Breckwoldt 4 and 24bl, voyata 7, Guzel Studio 8, vagabond54 10, Alfredo Cerra 11, KWSPhotography 16, Renata Sedmakova 17, Vorobiev Aleksey 19, kornilov007 20t, mircea dobre 20b, Kotsovolos Panagiotis 21t, Rvector 22, vvoe 24tl, Atomazul 25bl, Elnur 25br, Terry Kettlewell 26t, Olena Mykhaylova 29, stockelements 30t, Igorsky 31, majeczka 32t, Natali Glado 32bl, Artur Bogacki 32br, joreks 33tl, Capricorn Studio 33b, pashamba 34t, poo 34c, Ariyaphol Jiwalak 34b, Sander van der Werf 35t, MISHELLA 35br, Paul Broadbent 36, iulianmarcu 38tl, HelloRF Zcool 39tr, Travel Stock 38b, leungchopan 39br, thelefty 40, Rahhal 44, chombosan 45.

All design elements from Shutterstock.

First published in Great Britain in 2017 by Wayland

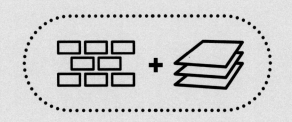

Printed and bound in China at WKT Company Ltd.

TABLE OF CONTENTS

STARTING OUT

The architects of the Lloyd's Building in London wanted to create a spacious, open-plan working space. They designed the building with pipes, elevators, and electricity cables on the outside to create more space inside.

STRUCTURES ARE ALL AROUND US, FROM HOUSES AND OFFICES TO HUGE SKYSCRAPERS AND BRIDGES. CREATING ANY BUILDING, WHETHER BIG OR SMALL, REQUIRES A LOT OF HARD WORK AND CAREFUL PLANNING.

When people decide to construct a new building, they have to go through a planning process. There are many important questions to be answered at every stage.

STEP 1

CONCEPT What is the purpose of the building? How big does it need to be? What features does it need?

STEP 2

DESIGN How will the building fulfill the aims set out in the concept? What will it look like? Will it stay up and be safe to live and work in?

STEP 3

CREATION How can the design be converted into a real building? How much of each material is needed? How long will it take to build?

PROJECT

- Choose a building in your neighborhood and think about its concept. Describe its purpose, features, and size.

- Why do you think its creators chose this concept?

- Do you think they were successful?

- What could be changed to make the building more useful or attractive?

IT TAKES A CREW OF PEOPLE WITH DIFFERENT SKILLS TO DESIGN AND MAKE A BUILDING.

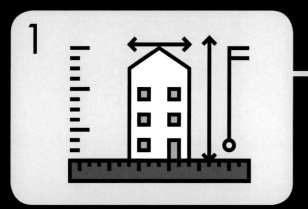

Architects use their creative skills to design and draw plans for the building. City planners check that the building will be a useful addition to the community.

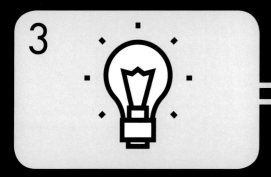

The architects work closely with structural engineers. Structural engineers use their knowledge of physics to make sure that the weight of the building will be properly supported. They also need to make sure that the building will be able to resist forces, such as wind.

Building services engineers plan systems for heating, cooling, and lighting the building.

TECHNOLOGY TALK

Today architects and engineers can use computer programs to plan and test buildings before they are constructed, preventing potential mistakes! In the past, architects and engineers could only rely on their knowledge and experience when designing buildings, which makes ancient structures even more impressive.

Finally, builders use their skills to construct the building.

MATERIALS

THERE ARE MANY THINGS TO CONSIDER WHEN CHOOSING A MATERIAL FOR A BUILDING. ARCHITECTS MAY PREFER CERTAIN MATERIALS FOR THEIR VISUAL APPEAL AND COST. THEY ALSO NEED TO THINK ABOUT WHETHER THEY WILL WORK WITH THEIR BUILDING'S DESIGN. ENGINEERS CONSIDER A MATERIAL'S STRENGTH AND SAFETY.

The first buildings were made from naturally occurring materials, such as wood, mud, and stone. Later, humans learned how to produce and use concrete, bricks, glass, and metal. Today we use a combination of different materials in new buildings, with heavy bricks and concrete for the structural elements and glass for the windows.

SCIENCE TALK

Pure metals, such as iron, don't usually make good building materials. They are easy to bend because their **atoms** are all the same size and can easily slide past each other. **Alloys**, such as steel, have atoms of different sizes. It is much harder for the structure of their atoms to change shape, so they make much stronger building materials.

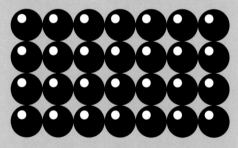

The atoms in iron are all the same size.

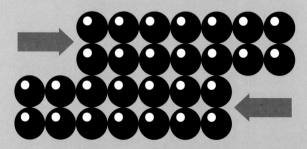

Iron will distort easily as the atoms slide past each other.

THINKING OUTSIDE THE BOX!

Sometimes traditional materials can be reinvented for modern designs. Instead of using large blocks of stone to construct walls, Japanese architect Kengo Kuma sometimes uses thin slices of stone to decorate the outside of his buildings.

In his design for the Asakusa Culture and Tourism Center in Japan, Kengo Kuma spaced thin slices of wood along the windows in different ways to offer more or less privacy to the rooms inside.

Today scientists are developing "smart materials" that can change in response to temperature, pressure, or moisture. One of the most incredible smart materials is self-healing concrete. When cracks appear in this type of concrete, it exposes tiny pods of bacteria and calcium to the air and rain. The bacteria in this concrete is activated by water. It then mixes with calcium to form limestone and closes up the cracks.

Graphene is a promising material made from carbon atoms arranged in honeycombs. It is incredibly thin, yet it is the strongest material in the world. Scientists believe that covering buildings with graphene paint helps with **insulation** and protects the walls against **corrosion**.

" ART TALK

The appearance of materials is also important when designing a new building. Architects often choose colors and textures that complement or contrast with each other. For example, rough, red bricks will stand out against smooth, gray metal.

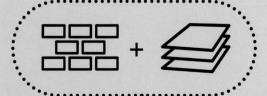

STRUCTURE

MAKING A BUILDING STAY UP REQUIRES CLEVER ENGINEERING, AS UNBALANCED FORCES ACTING ON A STRUCTURE CAN BRING IT CRASHING TO THE GROUND.

Gravity can be a serious risk to construction if it isn't managed properly. Weight is the force of a building's **mass** being pulled toward Earth by gravity. If the weight of a building pushes down harder than Earth's surface can resist upward, the building will sink into the ground. This is why it is important to construct buildings on solid, dry ground.

The famous Leaning Tower of Pisa in Italy was built on soft, unstable ground. It started leaning during construction in the 12th century.

ENGINEERING TALK

Underground **foundations** keep buildings from tipping over by turning forces. When a force, such as wind, puts pressure on the side of a building, the foundations resist and push back in the opposite direction. This balances the forces and stops the building from falling over.

HOW GRAVITY MAKES A WALL COLLAPSE

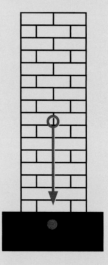
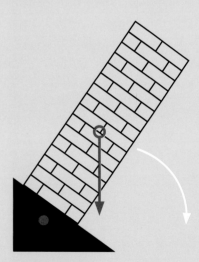

Gravity can also make buildings fall to one side. If a building's center of gravity is not above the center of its base, gravity will create a turning force called a moment. This force will push the building over.

Metal or wood **beams** are often built inside walls and floors to help structures **withstand** forces. An unsupported ceiling can only bear a small amount of weight from the floor above without caving in. Adding horizontal beams in the floor that run across to the walls means any weight placed on the ceiling is transferred sideways and will be supported by the stronger vertical walls.

THINKING OUTSIDE THE BOX!

Rectangles are not particularly strong shapes for building as they easily change shape or collapse if you push on their sides. If you add a diagonal beam across a rectangle, you create two triangles. This makes the rectangular wall much stronger because you cannot distort a triangle without breaking its beams.

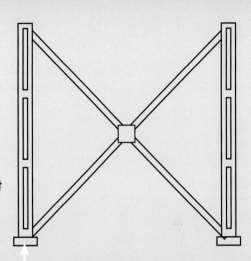

Adding two diagonal beams makes a rectangular wall even stronger because it is divided into four triangles instead of two.

ENGINEERING
TALK

▼ PUSH HERE   DISTORTS

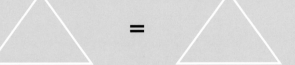

=

If you push on the side of a rectangle, it can change into a parallelogram without breaking its sides.

▼ PUSH HERE   NO CHANGE

=

If you push on the side of a triangle, it will only change shape if you exert enough force to break its sides.

PROJECT

- Make a triangle and a rectangle from sticky putty and toothpicks. Use a blob of sticky putty at each of the corners.

- How easy is it to distort the rectangle into a parallelogram?

- What happens if you add a diagonal toothpick across the rectangle?

- Are all types of triangles equally strong?

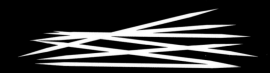

ARCHES AND DOMES

ALTHOUGH ARCHES AND DOMES LOOK FRAGILE, THEY CAN SUPPORT GREAT WEIGHT. THE SECRET TO A STRONG ARCH IS **COMPRESSION**—A SQUEEZING FORCE THAT SUPPORTS THE CURVE WITHOUT ANYTHING UNDERNEATH IT.

This Roman aqueduct in Segovia, Spain, is still standing today. There is little or no **mortar** bonding the stones together. The pieces hold each other in place.

Roman architects (see pages 20–21) used arches everywhere, from bridges and **aqueducts** to giant public buildings, such as the Colosseum in Rome, Italy. Because arches have an empty space in the center, they can be stacked to make tall walls that weigh much less than standard structures.

SCIENCE TALK

KEYSTONE

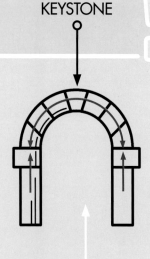

Instead of pushing straight down, the weight of an arch is pushed outward from the keystone (central stone) along the curve to the supports at each side. These supports push back, creating a compression force that keeps the arch from collapsing. However, this force is only created when the arch is complete, so arches need to be supported by a frame while they are being constructed.

PROJECT

- Build an arch from ice cubes.
- How could you stick the ice cubes together?
- How could you support the rest of the arch while you are adding new pieces?
- How could you change the shape of the ice cubes to make them fit together better?

THINKING OUTSIDE THE BOX!

If you rotate several arches around a central point, it creates a half-**sphere** shape, also known as a dome. Domes make dramatic ceilings or roofs and are often used in religious buildings. Like an arch, the weight of a dome is transferred outward to the edge of the curve. It is supported by the walls underneath, which push back, balancing the force.

OCULUS

The domed roof of the Pantheon in Rome has an oculus (hole) which provides natural light. Engineers carved intricate shapes known as coffers along the walls to reduce weight.

Modern **geodesic** domes are made from triangle-shaped pieces rather than a circle of arches. Each triangle is made from glass or plastic and is held in place by a metal frame. The metal structure distributes weight across the entire dome, which means that it does not need strong walls underneath for support.

SCALE AND PLANS

ONCE YOU HAVE THE IDEA FOR A BUILDING, YOU NEED TO DRAW YOUR PLANS SO THAT YOU CAN SHARE THEM WITH OTHER PEOPLE. ARCHITECTS PLAN THE INSIDE AND OUTSIDE OF BUILDINGS AHEAD OF TIME, SO NOTHING IS LEFT TO CHANCE.

It would be silly to draw a life-sized design for a building. Instead, architects draw smaller plans using **scale**. Scale drawings give an idea of how the final result will look. Inside plans are usually drawn in more detail than outside plans because architects need to make sure they have left enough space for rooms and furniture.

MATH TALK

In scale drawings, all measurements are reduced by the same amount. For example, a scale of 1:200 means that 1 inch on the page is 200 inches in real life. Similarly, 1 foot on the page would be 200 feet in real life. What is the scale shown in this image?

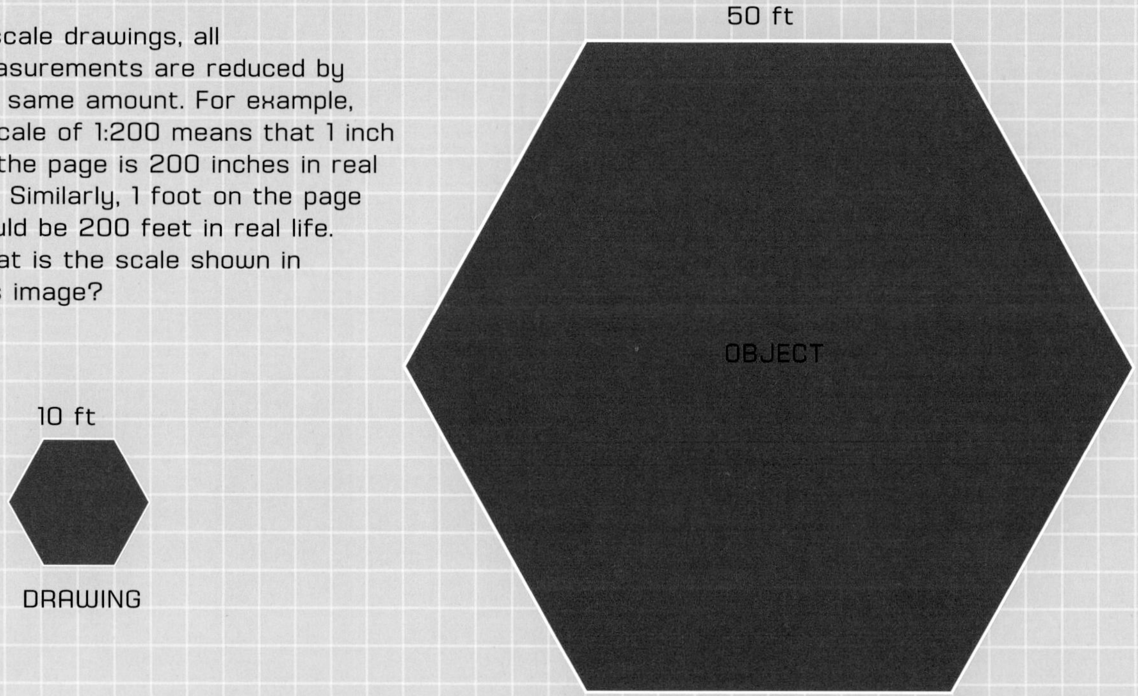

50 ft

OBJECT

10 ft

DRAWING

Architects do different types of drawing to show each part of a building. The inside of a building is often drawn as a floor plan. This is a flat overhead view with doors, windows, stairs, and furniture marked in place. Architects design plans for each floor of a building.

These plans show two floors in a house. How are the stairs, doors, and windows marked on the plan?

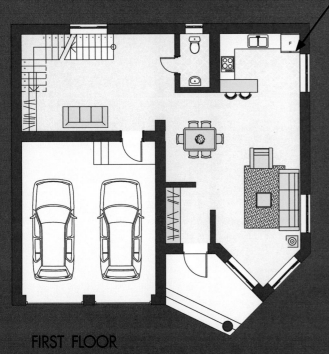

FIRST FLOOR

SECOND FLOOR

PROJECT

- With the help of an adult, measure the walls and furniture with a tape measure. Then choose a scale that best fits the page.

- Which scale will you use? How will you mark windows and doors?

- How detailed can you make your drawing with the scale you have chosen?

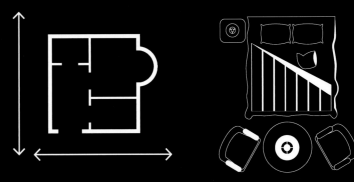

PERSPECTIVE

FLAT FLOOR PLANS ARE VERY USEFUL, BUT SOMETIMES WE NEED A CLEARER IMAGE OF HOW A BUILDING WILL LOOK IN REAL LIFE. DRAWING IN **PERSPECTIVE** ALLOWS US TO CREATE A 3D-VIEW OF A STRUCTURE ON A 2D-PIECE OF PAPER.

The general idea of perspective is to make objects appear on the page as they do in real life. To do this, nearby objects need to be drawn larger than faraway objects.

This photo uses one-point perspective. In drawings with one-point perspective, all horizontal lines that are **parallel** in real life, such as the top and bottom parts of the bridge, meet at one **vanishing point** on the **horizon** line. Although we know that the bridge is the same width all the way down, the bridge appears to get narrower in the photo because of perspective.

VANISHING POINT

HORIZON

parallel in real life

THINKING OUTSIDE THE BOX!

Painters have not always used perspective as we do today. They drew items to be taller or shorter depending on their importance, rather than their distance from the viewer. However, in the 15th and 16th centuries, people started trying to use math and science to understand the world. Taking a mathematical approach to art helped them understand perspective and apply it successfully to their artwork.

Leonardo da Vinci's *The Last Supper* was completed in the late 15th century and uses one-point perspective. Jesus' head is located at the vanishing point to make him stand out from the others.

Some architectural drawings use two-point perspective. This is a style of perspective in which horizontal lines meet at one of two vanishing points along the horizon line. All vertical lines stay parallel and never meet. If you are drawing a very tall building, you may need to use three-point perspective, in which two vanishing points are along the horizon, but the third is above or below the horizon.

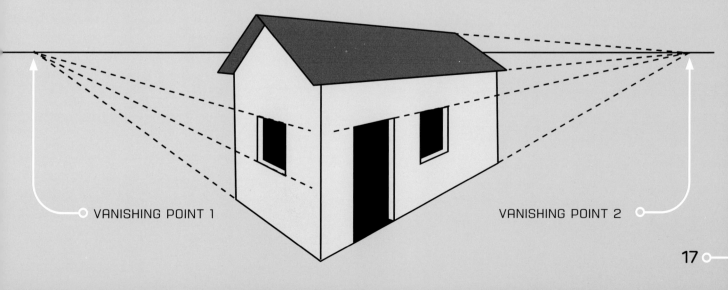

VANISHING POINT 1

VANISHING POINT 2

ANCIENT BUILDINGS

THE FIRST MAN-MADE STRUCTURES WERE PROBABLY MADE FROM WOOD, MUD, AND ANIMAL SKINS. THESE BUILDINGS HAVE SINCE DECOMPOSED, BUT SOME STONE BUILDINGS FROM ANCIENT CIVILIZATIONS STILL REMAIN, GIVING US A FASCINATING INSIGHT INTO EARLY ENGINEERING AND TECHNOLOGY.

Ancient builders made structures for some of the same reasons we do today. Most people lived in simple houses designed to keep them safe from the elements. Large, grand buildings were often constructed for rich people as a symbol of their power. The pyramids in Egypt served as tombs for the pharaohs (ancient Egyptian rulers). Super-sized religious buildings and worship sites, such as Stonehenge in England, were built for religious ceremonies and as a way to honor the gods.

" MATH TALK

The ancient Egyptians used math to design perfect pyramids. In order to make the top of each side meet in the center, they had to make the slope of each side exactly the same. The Egyptians achieved this by making each angle measure 51.4 degrees at the base. Then they calculated the angle at the top of each side. If all the angles inside a triangle must add up to 180 degrees, what should the top angle measure?

?

51.4 degrees

51.4 degrees

The Ziggurat of Ur was built by the Sumerians around 4,117 years ago in the area known today as Iraq. This mud brick temple originally measured over 30 m (70 to 100 feet) high, but only the lower levels remain today.

There are no written records of how ancient structures were built. It's hard to imagine how the creators of Stonehenge moved the giant blocks of stone into place without modern machines. Many wonder how the ancient Egyptians built the towering pyramids without cranes to lift the top pieces into place.

THINKING OUTSIDE THE BOX!

Some historians and engineers have come up with theories as to how ancient buildings were constructed. One theory is that the stones that make up Egypt's pyramids were pulled up flat ramps on sleds and then slotted into place. The stones used in Stonehenge may have been transported by rafts and giant sleds and then pulled into place using ropes. Some hands-on historians have even tried out their theories to prove that they are possible.

SCIENCE TALK

Scientists suspect that some of the rocks in Stonehenge came from western Wales—hundreds of miles away from the structure's site in England. Scientists confirmed this theory by studying crystals in Stonehenge's rocks, which were identical to rocks found only in western Wales.

GREEKS AND ROMANS

THE ANCIENT GREEKS AND ROMANS WERE SKILLED ARCHITECTS AND ENGINEERS. BOTH CIVILIZATIONS HAD IONIC ARCHITECTURAL STYLES THAT ARE STILL IN USE TODAY.

GREEK COLUMNS

Greek architects liked symmetry so they followed specific rules to make sure that all of their buildings looked similar. Columns with carved details were a key feature of Greek architecture. The three main styles of columns were Doric, Ionic, and Corinthian, which can easily be identified by their features.

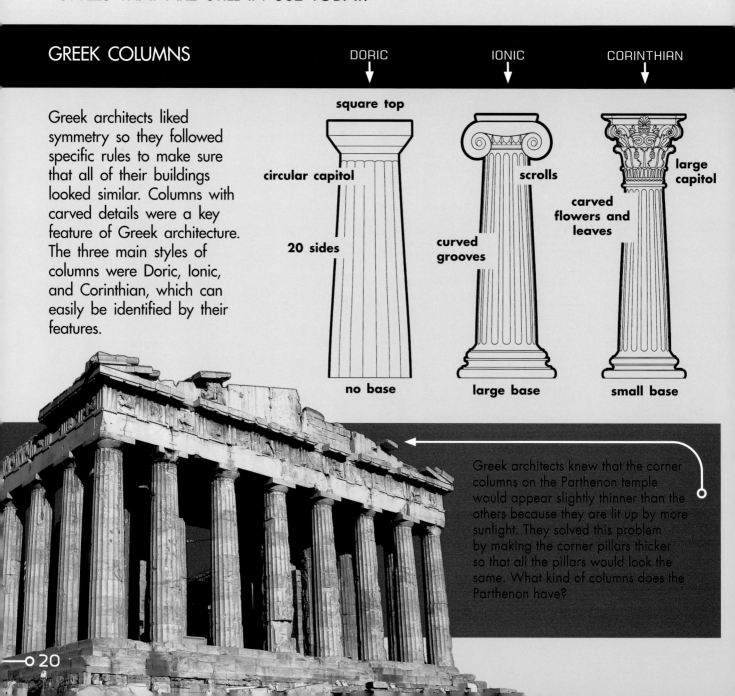

DORIC

IONIC

CORINTHIAN

square top

circular capitol

20 sides

no base

scrolls

curved grooves

large base

large capitol

carved flowers and leaves

small base

Greek architects knew that the corner columns on the Parthenon temple would appear slightly thinner than the others because they are lit up by more sunlight. They solved this problem by making the corner pillars thicker so that all the pillars would look the same. What kind of columns does the Parthenon have?

ENGINEERING *TALK*

As well as looking perfect, Greek buildings were highly functional. The Greeks were huge theater fans, and they studied how sound bounced off different surfaces to give their theaters incredible sound quality. The best sound quality was in the theater in Epidaurus, which held more than 12,000 people. Everyone in the theater, including the people in the back row, could hear something as quiet as paper ripping on stage!

The Romans' development of concrete gave them the freedom to create new types of structures. Instead of relying on columns to support a roof, they could make self-supporting domes and arches from concrete. The insides of buildings could be open and spacious, rather than dotted with tall pillars like Greek buildings.

THINKING OUTSIDE THE BOX!

Concrete wasn't a Roman invention, but the Romans spiced up the recipe by adding volcanic ash. The Romans didn't know that volcanic ash would give the concrete special properties, but since Italy is the only country in Europe with active volcanoes, they had plenty lying around! As it turned out, concrete made with ash did not crack easily and could set underwater—a lucky discovery based on trial and error. Some builders today are considering a return to Roman concrete because it is cheaper and lasts longer than modern concrete.

CASTLES AND CATHEDRALS

DURING THE MIDDLE AGES, LARGE, GRAND BUILDINGS SPRUNG UP ACROSS EUROPE. ROYALTY AND POWERFUL LORDS HAD TONS OF MONEY TO SPEND, AND THEY SPLURGED ON HOMES AND HUGE RELIGIOUS BUILDINGS.

Castles are probably the most iconic buildings of the Middle Ages. They were mainly defensive buildings built to protect the lord who controlled the surrounding land. But they were also symbols of power and wealth. Castles were designed with features that made them easier to defend, such as thick stone walls, arrow slits, battlements, towers, and a moat.

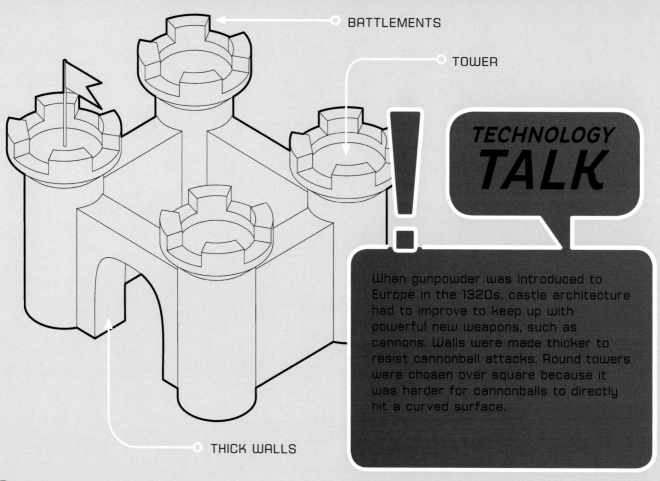

BATTLEMENTS

TOWER

THICK WALLS

TECHNOLOGY TALK

When gunpowder was introduced to Europe in the 1320s, castle architecture had to improve to keep up with powerful new weapons, such as cannons. Walls were made thicker to resist cannonball attacks. Round towers were chosen over square because it was harder for cannonballs to directly hit a curved surface.

While castle architecture favored practicality, medieval architects could let their creative juices flow when working on cathedrals. Elaborate designs were preferred because people wanted to create beautiful buildings as a sign of their devotion to the Christian religion. Medieval builders spent thousands of hours manually carving giant arches and impressive vaults to support high ceilings.

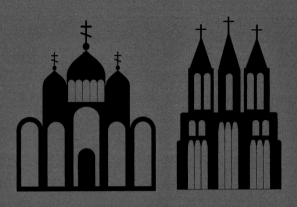

Work began on the Sagrada Família in 1882, but it is still unfinished! It is expected to be completed between 2026 and 2028.

" ART TALK

Cathedrals and grand churches are still being built today, long after the Middle Ages. Some modern religious buildings are inspired by trends in art. For example, when architect Antoni Gaudí designed the Sagrada Família in Barcelona, Spain, he combined Gothic and art nouveau styles with curved details inspired by nature. The Cathedral in Brasília, Brazil, has a modern design that was popular in the 1950s and 1960s. "

The Cathedral in Brasília combines traditional elements of religious buildings, such as stained-glass windows, with striking modern concrete columns.

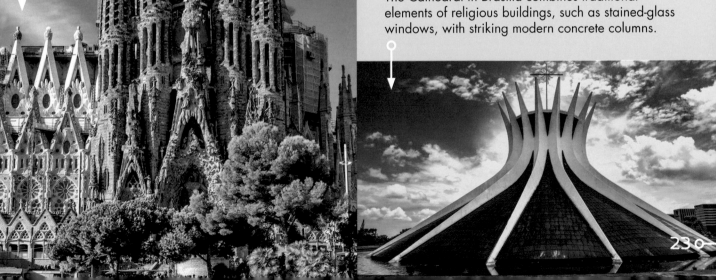

HALL OF FAME: ARCHITECTS

SOME OF THE MOST ICONIC BUILDINGS IN HISTORY ARE THE RESULTS OF THE CREATIVITY AND TECHNICAL SKILLS OF ARCHITECTS. BECAUSE THESE ARCHITECTS EMBRACED AND EXPERIMENTED WITH THE MATERIALS AND TECHNOLOGY AVAILABLE TO THEM, THEY ESTABLISHED ARCHITECTURAL STYLES THAT WERE UNIQUELY THEIRS.

MICHELANGELO (1475–1564)

Although Michelangelo is particularly well known for his sculptures and paintings, he was also a skilled architect. His design for the egg-shaped dome of St Peter's Basilica in Rome, was a feat of engineering. The church's egg-shaped dome puts less pressure on the base than a half-spherical dome.

ANTONI GAUDÍ (1852–1926)

Most of Gaudí's ornate creations are located in or near Barcelona. His buildings were inspired by nature, not just in their decoration, but also in their structure. They have columns, arches, and roofs that were designed to mimic natural supporting structures, such as bones and branches.

SIR CHRISTOPHER WREN (1632–1723)

After the Great Fire of London in 1666, there was a huge demand for architects to repair and rebuild the city. Wren was talented and in the right place at the right time. He helped rebuild St. Paul's Cathedral and many churches, leaving his permanent signature on the London skyline.

LOUIS SULLIVAN (1856–1924)

The development of **mass-produced** steel in the 19th century inspired American architect Louis Sullivan to use huge steel **girders** to support the weight of his buildings. Freed from the restrictions of load-bearing walls, Sullivan built higher than ever before, creating some of the world's first skyscrapers! Sullivan is well known for the saying "form follows function." This became a popular principle among 20th-century architects who believed that the purpose of a building should be the starting point for its design.

The Guggenheim Museum in Bilbao, Spain, was designed by Frank Gehry.

FRANK GEHRY (BORN 1929)

Gehry's style is sometimes described as "deconstructed" because his buildings tend to be free-form shapes. His work does not always follow the rule of "form over function" because many elements of his buildings serve no purpose other than decoration. However, the overall effect is undeniably spectacular.

Zaha Hadid designed the stunning Heydar Aliyev Center in Azerbaijan.

ZAHA HADID (1950–2016)

This Iraqi-born, British architect brought a distinctive futuristic curved style to all of her projects, including the 2012 London Olympics Aquatics Centre. Modern computer software allowed her to figure out how to engineer and construct her characteristic gravity-defying buildings.

HOUSES

HOUSES MAY SEEM ORDINARY, BUT THEY ARE SOME OF THE MOST IMPORTANT BUILDINGS ON EARTH. EVERY PERSON IN THE WORLD DESERVES A SHELTER AND A PLACE TO CALL HOME.

In Europe, Iron Age houses were constructed from branches and dried plants.

For most of human history, houses were simple one-story structures. Holes were cut out of the walls for light and ventilation. They were covered with animal skins or wooden shutters until sheet glass became more readily available around 300 years ago. It was only in the 20th century that most homes in the western world were fitted with running water, electricity, and indoor toilets.

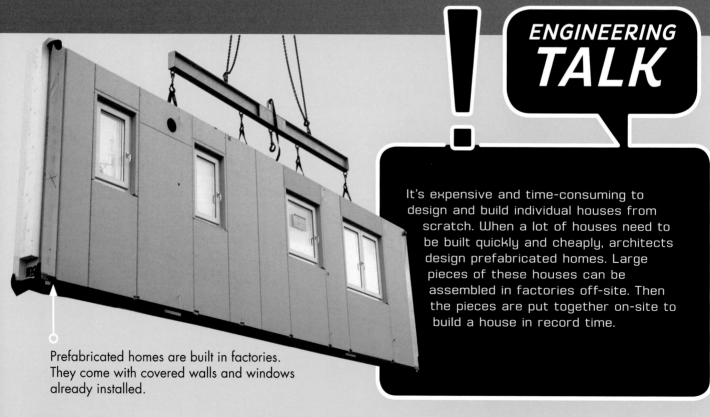

Prefabricated homes are built in factories. They come with covered walls and windows already installed.

ENGINEERING TALK

It's expensive and time-consuming to design and build individual houses from scratch. When a lot of houses need to be built quickly and cheaply, architects design prefabricated homes. Large pieces of these houses can be assembled in factories off-site. Then the pieces are put together on-site to build a house in record time.

As the world's population grows, it has become more difficult to find space to build housing. Building upward is much more space-efficient than building outward. That's why tall apartment buildings are commonly built in cities where land is expensive and hard to come by.

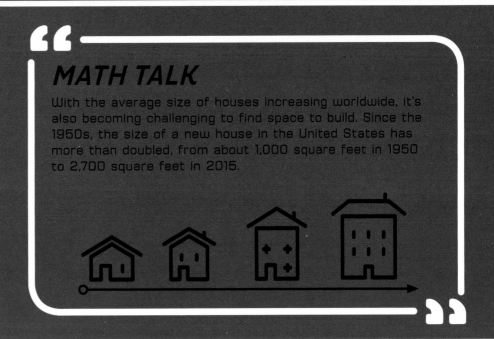

MATH TALK

With the average size of houses increasing worldwide, it's also becoming challenging to find space to build. Since the 1950s, the size of a new house in the United States has more than doubled, from about 1,000 square feet in 1950 to 2,700 square feet in 2015.

A square foot is a square that measures one foot by one foot. A cubic foot is a cube that measures one foot along each side. Given the measurements shown below, can you figure out the size of these bedrooms and closet in square feet? How big is your bedroom or classroom in square feet?

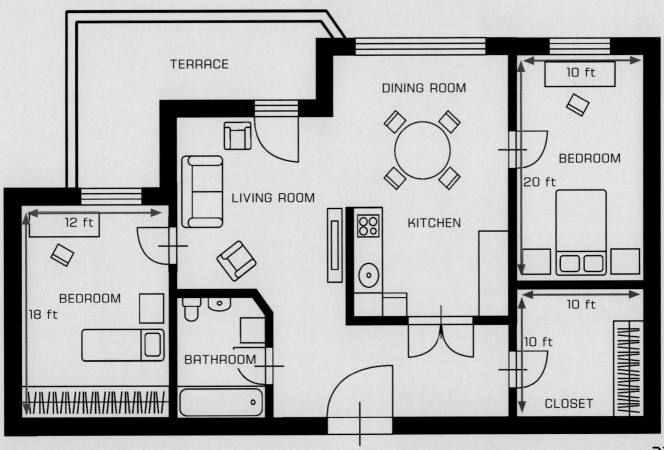

ECO-FRIENDLY BUILDINGS

OUR GROWING WORLD POPULATION IS PUTTING MORE PRESSURE ON RESOURCES, SUCH AS BUILDING MATERIALS AND THE FOSSIL FUELS BURNED TO POWER OUR BUILDINGS. MAKING BUILDINGS MORE ECO-FRIENDLY COULD BE PART OF THE SOLUTION.

Using **renewable** resources, such as wood, is a simple way to make construction more eco-friendly. The resources needed to make these materials can be regrown in several years, but rock and metals are non-renewable. Some architects are also designing buildings using recycled materials, such as stone or bricks, from abandoned or damaged buildings. This reduces waste and cuts down on the energy used to create new building materials.

THINKING OUTSIDE THE BOX!

In addition to traditional building materials, there are many unusual materials that can be reused and recycled in new buildings. Plastic bottles and egg cartons, for example, can be used to line walls as insulation.

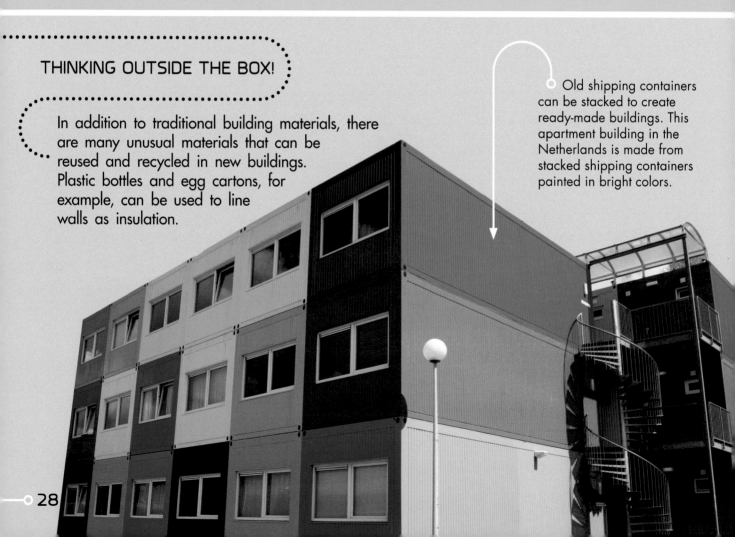

Old shipping containers can be stacked to create ready-made buildings. This apartment building in the Netherlands is made from stacked shipping containers painted in bright colors.

PROJECT

- Test household materials to see if they make good insulators. Place three small plastic cups inside three large, clean yogurt containers. Pack a different material, such as paper or cotton balls, around the side of each cup inside two of the yogurt containers. Place nothing in the third container. Put an ice cube in each of the three cups. The container in which the ice takes the longest to melt contains the best insulation material.

- Before you start your test, which material do you think will make the best insulator?

- Why?

- What other materials could you test?

Architects can also make buildings more eco-friendly by designing them to consume fewer resources than traditional buildings. The easiest way to do this is to make buildings as small as possible, while still allowing enough space for them to be functional. This means that less energy will be needed to heat and cool the buildings.

TECHNOLOGY TALK

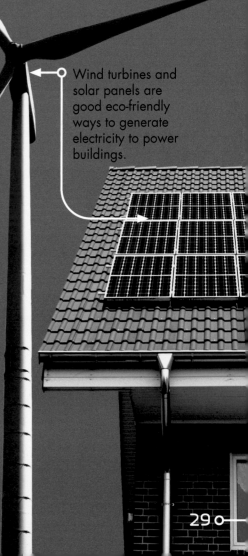

Wind turbines and solar panels are good eco-friendly ways to generate electricity to power buildings.

There are many technological devices that can make buildings more eco-friendly, such as solar panels. Solar panels can be placed on the roof of a building to convert energy from the sun into energy that can be used to power lights, heating, and other electronic items. Some eco-friendly houses also have wind turbines to generate energy. Others use systems that recycle rain or used water from showers and dishwashers to flush their toilets.

SKYSCRAPERS

CITIES AROUND THE WORLD
ARE FILLED WITH SHINY SKYSCRAPERS
THAT CREATE BEAUTIFUL CITYSCAPES.
THESE TOWERING BUILDINGS STAY
UP IN THE AIR THANKS TO SMART
ENGINEERING AND DESIGN.

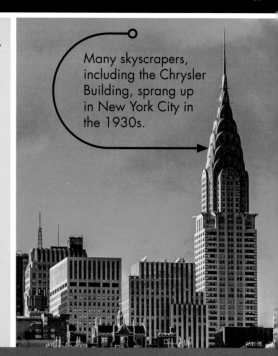

Many skyscrapers, including the Chrysler Building, sprang up in New York City in the 1930s.

As thousands of people flocked to U.S. cities in the second half of the 19th-century, offices and homes were in short supply. As a result, land in the city centers became costly. The solution was to build upward, and the skyscraper was born!

Skyscrapers have popped up in many different countries. This diagram shows the eight tallest buildings in the world as of 2017. How much taller is the Burj Khalifa than the Shanghai Tower?

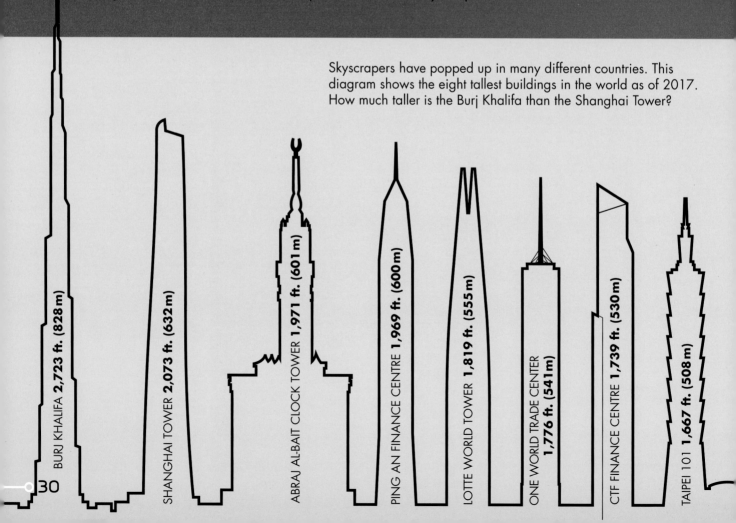

BURJ KHALIFA 2,723 ft. (828 m)

SHANGHAI TOWER 2,073 ft. (632 m)

ABRAJ AL-BAIT CLOCK TOWER 1,971 ft. (601 m)

PING AN FINANCE CENTRE 1,969 ft. (600 m)

LOTTE WORLD TOWER 1,819 ft. (555 m)

ONE WORLD TRADE CENTER 1,776 ft. (541 m)

CTF FINANCE CENTRE 1,739 ft. (530 m)

TAIPEI 101 1,667 ft. (508 m)

THINKING OUTSIDE THE BOX!

The first skyscrapers had incredibly thick outer walls to support the weight of the top floors. But this took away usable space from the bottom of the building. So, in the center, architects began adding steel structures that support the weight of the building.

SCIENCE TALK

Designing sky-high structures can be tricky because every story adds extra weight. Gravity makes this weight pull down on the base of the building. The weight needs to be balanced so that it doesn't make the building collapse.

PROJECT

- Build your own skyscraper using dry spaghetti noodles and marshmallows. Push the spaghetti into the marshmallows to join pieces together.

  - What shape should the base of the skyscraper be?

    - How can you stabilize your tower?

      - What could you change to make your skyscraper even taller?

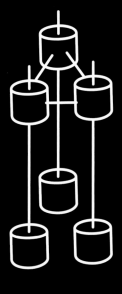

Because the outside walls of a skyscraper don't carry any weight, they can be made from glass or thin metal, giving the buildings the iconic shiny look that we know today.

31

HALL OF FAME: LANDMARKS

THE WORLD'S MOST FAMOUS LANDMARKS ARE OFTEN BUILDINGS, SUCH AS THE TAJ MAHAL, THE EIFFEL TOWER, AND THE EMPIRE STATE BUILDING. THESE BUILDINGS WERE CONSTRUCTED AT DIFFERENT TIMES, FROM DIFFERENT MATERIALS, AND FOR DIFFERENT REASONS, BUT THEY ARE ALL BELOVED FEATS OF ENGINEERING AND ARCHITECTURE.

EIFFEL TOWER

The Eiffel Tower in Paris, France, gets its name from its designer, Gustave Eiffel, who was a skilled bridge engineer. His experience designing bridges strongly influenced his design of the Eiffel Tower, which is made of a **lattice** of wrought iron, just like many bridges.

HAGIA SOPHIA

The Hagia Sophia in Istanbul, Turkey, was completed in AD 537 as Christian church. Despite its colossal size and ornate details, the church took only six years to build.

LEANING TOWER OF PISA

Most flawed buildings have been demolished or abandoned, but the Leaning Tower of Pisa in Italy is celebrated for its unintentional tilt. Over time, the tilt became more extreme, but the tower has now been stabilized by removing soil from underneath the higher side.

EMPIRE STATE BUILDING

Inexpensive steel and a desire for more office space in New York City inspired the construction of the Empire State Building in 1930. At 1,454 feet (443 m) tall, it stands out from the other skyscrapers in the New York skyline. Its Art Deco architecture, with setbacks (stepped sections) exaggerating its height and giving it an elegant tapered shape.

SETBACK

SETBACK

SETBACK

ANGKOR WAT

Angkor Wat in Cambodia is the largest religious monument in the world. Featuring pointed towers, its structure is designed to represent a sacred Hindu mountain. It is decorated with carved scenes from Hindu mythology.

TAJ MAHAL

Built in the mid-17th century, the Taj Mahal is a large, grand tomb in Agra, India. Its simple elegance comes from its perfect symmetry, pure ivory color, and balance of curved domes and straight pillars. It was built in the Mughal style, which combines elements of Indian, Persian, and Islamic architecture.

HALL OF FAME: PUBLIC BUILDINGS

MOST CITIES HAVE LARGE BUILDINGS DESIGNED FOR PUBLIC USE, FROM STADIUMS AND THEATERS TO AIRPORTS AND PARKING GARAGES. WHEN A BUILDING IS GOING TO BE VISITED BY THOUSANDS OF PEOPLE, IT'S IMPORTANT TO PLAN EXACTLY HOW IT WILL BE USED BECAUSE PROBLEMS COULD QUICKLY GET OUT OF HAND WITH SO MANY VISITORS.

ADOLFO SUÁREZ MADRID–BARAJAS AIRPORT

The main part of this airport in Madrid, Spain, was built in 1927. But its fourth terminal, which was finished in 2006, is its most exciting feature. The architects of Terminal 4 used bamboo in its construction. Glass panels along the walls and skylights on the roof let in natural light.

NATIONAL STADIUM, SINGAPORE

Rain can spoil even the most thrilling sporting event, so the architects of the National Stadium in Singapore came up with the perfect solution—the world's largest retractable dome roof. Giant panels, weighing thousands of pounds, can slide together to cover the roof if the clouds turn gray.

PARC DES CÉLESTINS

There's no reason why parking garages can't be designed in attractive and unusual ways. This underground parking garage in Lyon, France, was built around a hollow central cylinder. A rotating mirror in the center reflects light through the arches on each level and lights up the entire building.

SYDNEY OPERA HOUSE

This landmark concert hall in Sydney, Australia, can hold nearly 6,000 guests in its six theaters. It took architect Jørn Utzon and his team several years to figure out how to make the roof's now-iconic shells. Finally, Utzon realized that each shell could be created from the same sphere-shaped mold.

WORLD TRADE CENTER TRANSPORTATION HUB

This train station in New York City opened in 2016 to replace the station that was destroyed in the 9/11 terrorist attacks. On street level, there is a dramatic glass-paned structure, known as the Oculus, which lets in light. Inside are several airy open-plan levels with platforms for trains.

BRIDGES

BUILDING BRIDGES IS A COMPLICATED FEAT OF ENGINEERING. DESIGNERS HAVE TO FIGURE OUT HOW TO MAKE A HEAVY STRUCTURE CROSS A GREAT DISTANCE WITH LITTLE TO NO SUPPORT UNDERNEATH.

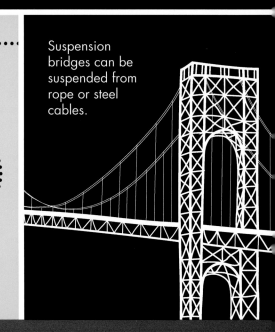

Suspension bridges can be suspended from rope or steel cables.

Early bridges were made from stones, ropes, wood, and concrete. During the Industrial Revolution, metalworking techniques improved and people developed ways of producing large amounts of cast iron and steel. Having access to these materials allowed engineers to design and build much larger bridges with different designs.

The Iron Bridge across the River Severn in England was the world's first arch bridge made of cast iron.

Unlike buildings, whose weight is supported by the ground pushing back against them, bridges generally have nothing underneath them to push back against gravity. If their weight isn't carefully balanced in other ways, they will come crashing to the ground. To keep a bridge in the air, engineers harness compression (pushing) and tension (pulling) forces to safely distribute the bridge's weight.

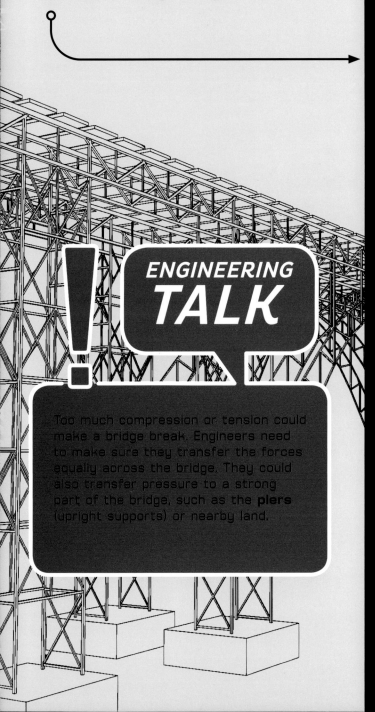

ENGINEERING TALK

Too much compression or tension could make a bridge break. Engineers need to make sure they transfer the forces equally across the bridge. They could also transfer pressure to a strong part of the bridge, such as the **piers** (upright supports) or nearby land.

Types of Bridges

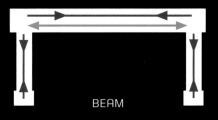

BEAM

ARCH

SUSPENSION

CABLE-STAY

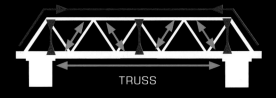

TRUSS

CANTILEVER

⬛ Tension   ⬛ Compression

MANY BRIDGES HAVE BECOME FAMOUS LANDMARKS, ATTRACTING TOURISTS WHO MARVEL AT THEIR ARCHITECTURE AND ENGINEERING. THEIR DESIGNS COMBINE ELEMENTS OF DIFFERENT BRIDGE TYPES DEPENDING ON THEIR FUNCTION, SIZE, AND LOCATION.

HANGZHOU BAY BRIDGE

At 22 miles (36 km) in length, the Hangzhou Bay Bridge on the east coast of China is one of the longest bridges in the world. This cable-stayed bridge is so long that it even has a service station in the middle, in case drivers need a break!

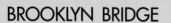

BROOKLYN BRIDGE

The Brooklyn Bridge in New York City is a combination of a cable-stayed and a suspension bridge. Instead of getting divers to work on the piers underwater, the piers were built on top of floating wooden boxes. These boxes eventually sank down to the bottom of the river due to the weight of construction above. The builders then worked inside the wooden boxes to attach the piers to the riverbed.

GOLDEN GATE BRIDGE

This suspension bridge in San Francisco, California, can sway from side to side in the wind. This isn't a design flaw, though. It's a feature that stops the bridge from bending and snapping in the high winds that blow in off the Pacific Ocean.

HALL OF FAME: BRIDGES

PONT DU GARD

This classic Roman aqueduct and bridge in southern France dates back to the 1st century. It was built to supply the city of Nîmes with water. The Pont du Gard is made up of more than 55,000 tons (50,000 tonnes) of limestone cut from a nearby quarry. Some parts of the bridge are made from pieces of limestone that were cut so accurately that no mortar was needed to join them together.

GATESHEAD MILLENNIUM BRIDGE

This bridge in Newcastle, England, is one of only three tilting bridges in the world. In a movement that looks like an eye blinking, the lower part of the bridge can swing up to let boats pass under it. The bridge was built off-site and lifted into place in one piece by a floating crane.

AKASHI KAIKYO BRIDGE

The designers of the Akashi Kaikyo Bridge—the longest suspension bridge in the world—knew they were in for a challenge from the start. The bridge's location in southern Japan often experiences earthquakes and strong winds. However, they didn't anticipate an earthquake during construction that moved the towers about 32 inches (80 cm) apart! They drew on their engineering experience to find a solution—making the bridge slightly longer than planned.

TUNNELS

BUILDING A TUNNEL SOUNDS SIMPLE. AFTER ALL, IT'S JUST AN UNDERGROUND TUBE! BUT TUNNELS ARE ACTUALLY VERY CHALLENGING TO BUILD BECAUSE ENGINEERS HAVE TO FIGURE OUT HOW TO BALANCE THE FORCES THAT ARE TRYING TO MAKE THE TUNNEL CAVE IN.

Tunnels have many uses, from carrying water or sewage underground to providing transportation routes under mountains or busy cities. The method of constructing a tunnel depends on the type of rock that it is going through. It's much harder to dig through hard rock than soft rock, but tunnels made in soft rock are more likely to collapse.

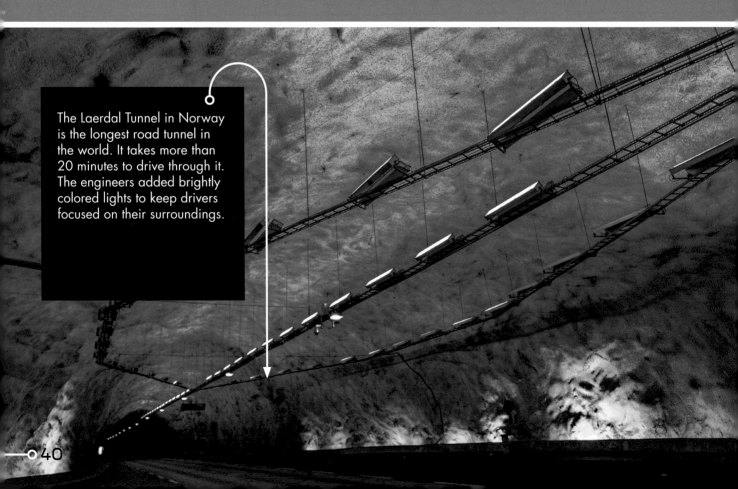

The Laerdal Tunnel in Norway is the longest road tunnel in the world. It takes more than 20 minutes to drive through it. The engineers added brightly colored lights to keep drivers focused on their surroundings.

THINKING OUTSIDE THE BOX!

In 1860 work began on the London Underground, the first subway system in the world. At that time, tunnel engineering was quite basic. To create the tunnels for the subway, workers used the cut and cover method. This involved digging a trench, building an arch roof over it, and then rebuilding the street on top. The tunnel shield—a temporary structure that supports a tunnel while it is being excavated—was invented in the 1860s. After that, builders were able to work entirely underground and dig much deeper tunnels.

SCIENCE TALK

To balance the pressure of the surrounding rock and soil pushing in, tunnels need to have a strong lining that will push outward and balance the forces. This prevents the tunnel from caving in. Tunnels are usually lined with stone, iron, or concrete because these materials can withstand strong forces.

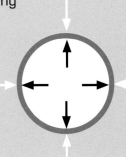

TECHNOLOGY TALK

Builders today dig tunnels using giant drills with rotating circular heads that slice into the rock. The rock and soil that are cut away fall to the back of the machine and are pushed out behind it. The drill can also place supports as it cuts away the rock to stop the tunnel from collapsing.

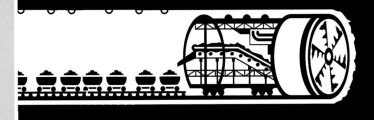

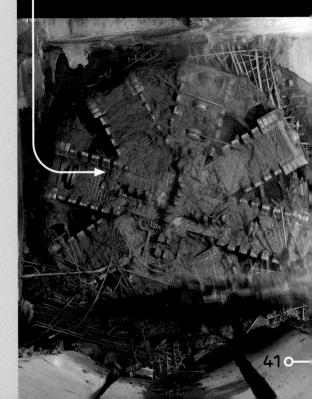

This giant tunnel-cutting drill is creating a tunnel for a new subway line.

WHEN THINGS GO WRONG

TODAY SOFTWARE CAN PREDICT IF BUILDINGS ARE STRUCTURALLY SOUND BEFORE CONSTRUCTION, BUT THERE IS ALWAYS A RISK THAT SOMETHING MIGHT GO WRONG.

One of the most dramatic engineering failures happened on the Tacoma Narrows Bridge in Washington State in 1940. During high winds, the cables on the suspension bridge twisted and snapped, making the beam of the bridge crumble. The Tacoma Narrows Bridge eventually collapsed into the river below.

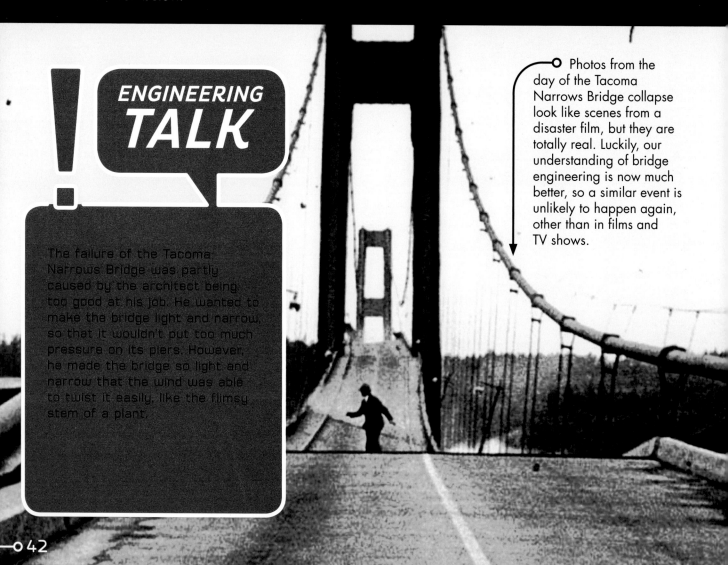

ENGINEERING TALK

The failure of the Tacoma Narrows Bridge was partly caused by the architect being too good at his job. He wanted to make the bridge light and narrow, so that it wouldn't put too much pressure on its piers. However, he made the bridge so light and narrow that the wind was able to twist it easily, like the flimsy stem of a plant.

Photos from the day of the Tacoma Narrows Bridge collapse look like scenes from a disaster film, but they are totally real. Luckily, our understanding of bridge engineering is now much better, so a similar event is unlikely to happen again, other than in films and TV shows.

Some problems are much more easily avoided because the architects really should know better. London's Walkie-Talkie Building, which was completed in 2014, made headlines when it melted a car on the street below! Apparently when the architects decided on a shiny surface for the building, they didn't consider how it would reflect sunlight down to the pavement. The building has since been covered with a special nonreflective film.

SCIENCE *TALK*

The Walkie-Talkie Building has a concave shape, which focuses the reflected rays of sunlight into a small area. This makes the sunlight much hotter than typical rays—up to 160 degrees Fahrenheit (70 degrees Celsius).

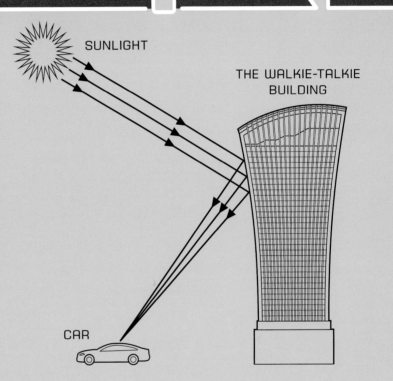

SUNLIGHT

THE WALKIE-TALKIE BUILDING

CAR

THINKING OUTSIDE THE BOX!

Computer programs are mainly used to anticipate and solve structural problems, but they can also help with other details. When architects created a computer model for London's new City Hall, they realized they had problems with sound bouncing around the 1,600-foot (500-m) tall open circular staircase. By making changes to the model in the program, the architects figured out how to solve the problem by adapting the stairs to trap sound. This saved them from making expensive, time-consuming repairs after construction was finished.

HOSTILE CONDITIONS

SOME BUILDINGS MUST WITHSTAND HARSH WEATHER CONDITIONS, SUCH AS STRONG WINDS AND EXTREME TEMPERATURES. IN PARTS OF THE WORLD THAT ARE LOCATED ALONG **FAULT LINES**, BUILDINGS ALSO HAVE TO BE ADAPTED TO DEAL WITH THE THREAT OF EARTHQUAKES.

Good insulation helps prevent people from roasting in very high temperatures and shivering in freezing weather. However, wind is much harder to control and can pose a serious threat to tall buildings. Tall buildings can sometimes also create wind problems for people at ground level. When wind hits the building and travels down its side, strong gusts of wind are blasted to the building's base.

ENGINEERING TALK

The Burj Khalifa in Dubai is covered in a heat-resistant material to stop the desert heat from pouring into the building.

All tall buildings are designed to sway gently in the wind. If a building tries to resist the force of the wind, it is more likely to crack than if it is able to move a little with the wind. However, very strong winds can push buildings over entirely. To prevent this, in very windy areas architects add strong internal supports to the center of buildings to resist these large forces.

A popular way to earthquake-proof a building is to isolate the foundation from the rest of the building. This lets the foundation move without moving the building above. Taipei 101 in Taiwan has a giant **pendulum** inside. This helps balance the forces by swaying in a direction opposite to the direction the building wants to move.

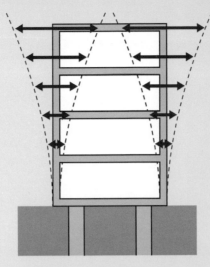

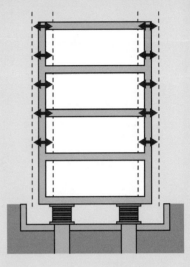

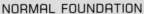

NORMAL FOUNDATION

ISOLATED FOUNDATION

SCIENCE TALK

This diagram shows the difference in movement of a normal building compared to an earthquake-proofed building with an isolated foundation.

Scientists are often inspired by the natural world. In their research to learn how to protect buildings from earthquakes, they are studying mussels to see how they use fibers to attach themselves to rocks underwater. Some of these fibers are rigid to keep a tight hold on the rock. Others are flexible so that they don't break in the crashing waves. Scientists believe that a similar approach may help buildings withstand earthquakes.

PROJECT

- Design an earthquake-resistant building using Legos®. Try three different designs and see which is sturdiest when you shake the base.

- How does each building react when you shake the base?

- What strength of shake can each building resist?

- Which shapes of building are better at resisting movement?

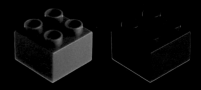

GLOSSARY

alloy (AL-oi)—a mixture of two or more metals

aqueduct (AK-wuh-duhkt)—a large bridge built to carry water over rivers and valleys

atom (AT-uhm)—the smallest part of matter that determines all of its properties

beam (BEEM)—a piece of wood, metal, or concrete used to support weight in a structure

compression (kuhm-PRE-shuhn)—stress on a structure from a force pushing or pressing against it

corrosion (kuh-ROH-shuhn)—the act of wearing away by a chemical reaction

fault line (FAWLT LYN)—a crack in the earth where two plates meet; earthquakes often occur along faults

foundation (foun-DAY-shuhn)—a base on which something rests or is built

geodesic (jee-uh-DES-ik DOHM)—a dome made of light straight structural elements

girder (GUR-dur)—a large, heavy beam made of steel or concrete and used in construction

gravity (GRAV-uh-tee)—a force that pulls objects together

horizon (huh-RYE-zuhn)—the line where the sky and the earth or sea seem to meet

insulation (in-suh-LAY-shun)—a material that stops heat, sound, or cold from entering or escaping

lattice (LAT-iss)—a pattern formed by strips that cross each other diagonally

mass (MASS)—the amount of material in an object

mass-produce (mas-pruh-DOOS)—to make large amounts of identical things with machines in a factory

mortar (MOR-tur)—a mixture of lime, sand, water, and cement that is used for building

parallel (PA-ruh-lel)—an equal distance apart at all points

pendulum (PEN-dyuh-luhm)—a weight that moves from side to side at a steady rate

perspective (pur-SPEK-tiv)—a way of drawing things so that distant objects are smaller than closer ones

pier (PEER)—a pillar that supports a bridge

renewable (ri-NOO-uh-buhl)—restored or replaced by natural processes; something that does not run out

scale (SKALE)—the ratio between the size of an object in a drawing and its size in real life

sphere (SFEER)—a solid round form like that of a basketball or globe

symmetry (SIM-i-tree)—the same on both sides of a center line

vanishing point (VAN-ish-ing POYNT)—a point in a drawing where parallel lines appear to meet

withstand (with-STAND)—to stand strongly against something, such as high winds

FURTHER READING

Howell, Izzi. *Extraordinary Buildings*. Exceptional Engineering. North Mankato, Minn.: Capstone Press, 2019.

Spray, Sally. *Bridges*. Awesome Engineering. North Mankato, Minn.: Capstone Press, 2018.

Ventura, Marne. *Building Skyscrapers*. Engineering Challenges. Mendota Heights, Minn.: North Star Editions, 2017.

INTERNET SITES

Use FactHound to find Internet sites related to this book.

Visit www.facthound.com

Just type in 9781543532241 and go.

Check out projects, games and lots more at
www.capstonekids.com

QUIZ

- **What is a geodesic dome?**
- **In a 1:10 scale, what size does 5 inches on the page represent in real life?**
- **Name a renewable building material and a non-renewable building material.**
- **Which two main forces must be balanced to keep a bridge safely in the air?**

INDEX

QUIZ ANSWERS

- A dome made from triangle-shaped pieces

- 50 inches

- Some renewable materials include wood and clay. Non-renewable materials include metal, rock, and plastic.

- Compression and tension